The 2013
BCS National
Championship

The 2013 BCS National Championship

A Reflection on America's Moral Equivalent of War, Occasioned by the Latest Meeting on the Gridiron of the Crimson Tide and Notre Dame

BY H. BRANDT AYERS

NEWSOUTH BOOKS

Montgomery

NewSouth Books
105 S. Court Street
Montgomery, AL 36104

Copyright © 2012 by H. Brandt Ayers
All rights reserved under International and Pan-American
Copyright Conventions. Published in the United States
by NewSouth Books, a division of NewSouth, Inc.,
Montgomery, Alabama.

ISBN 978-1-60306-273-2 (paperback)
ISBN 978-1-60306-274-9 (ebook)

Printed in the United States of America

The Early History

A s 2012 drew to a close, football fans awaited their annual abundance of college bowl games. If any needed justification for settling on the couch for hour after hour of watching, they could take heart—the sport means more than they may realize.

College football may be destined for an echo of the Reformation and the Thirty Years War as Protestant Alabama and Catholic Notre Dame compete for dominance. The next great battle between the two storied combatants was set for the 2013 BCS Championship on January 7, but the legacies of the two programs suggest prolonged warfare. Meanwhile, both keep an eye out for an evangelical insurgency on the distant horizon, where yet another pretender for national prominence rises from the foothills of Virginia: the Christian soldiers of Liberty University, which hopes not only to win a national title but the nation's soul.

All the expected sound and fury is to be taken seriously, because college football is not just a sport. It is America's cultural dynamo, the only one of our organized sports that taps into the martial spirit and evokes the fervor of religious faith (elsewhere in the world, the equivalent is that other football, what we call soccer). Further, college football has been a fulcrum of social change in the U.S.; its schemes date back to Hannibal; and some of its themes are drawn from military history and Shakespeare's tragedies.

How did such a tangle of art, history, emotions and intellect become embedded in a single sport? It evolved from rugby and has undergone various improvisations and mutations. Its passion arises from many sources—more acutely felt in the South with its bitter memories of defeat, isolation and scorn—but wellsprings of passion flow from school spirit, the pain of defeat and joy of victory, the awe inspired by wit and will pushing, striving, faking to overwhelm or outdo a similarly endowed opponent. Its purpose is not to entertain, though it does; its purpose is to win—an elemental motivator in humankind. It is a passion so flexed and fed in some schools it reaches the point of collegiate jingoism. I will not name names.

My first comprehension that there was an organized logic to the game came while sitting on a footstool before my Dad's big red leather chair in the library. With the stub of an old copy pencil, which Dad, the late Col. Harry M. Ayers, used for polishing his Sunday editorials in the *Anniston Star*, he drew a diagram of the 22 players and explained what each did. Next in my arc of discovery was when I reached a certain age and was invited to accompany the grown-ups to the cathedral—a stadium whose very name was mythic: Legion Field—where heroic figures in crimson fought for the honor of school, state and posterity. It was a benchmark experience—a Protestant Bar Mitzvah. However, it was at a New England prep school, the Wooster School in Danbury, Connecticut, that I was taught the moral aspects of the game. We were not merely encouraged but required to work or join a sports team. I chose football. What we learned were certain truths of life: the value of giving and taking solid licks, cooperation, and teamwork; the democratic leveling of seniors and prefects with underclassmen; the reality that some have greater skills than your own; the satisfaction of striving to perfect one's own talent; the idle cheapness of boasting; the discovery that defeat is possible and can be borne with dignity.

During my college and early professional years, Dad and I attended many games together; he in a tan overcoat with the scent of pipe tobacco. These memories are part of the cluster of emotions that go deeper than fan loyalty, into the realm of patriotism. A final memory came after he had a stroke in 1964 and was confined to a convalescent hospital. He had not spoken for weeks when I visited him after attending a game at Legion Field. Leaning down, I took his warm hand and said, "Dad, we whipped the hell out of Georgia today." He squeezed my hand.

Emotions like these, personalized to the individual's team and family, spiral like DNA through the nervous system of college football fans.

By comparison, NCAA rules changes seem pretty mundane, and they are. One recent change moved the kickoff from the 30-yard line to the 35, to make touchbacks more frequent and runbacks more infrequent. So be it. Kickoff returns invite high-velocity collisions when injuries occur.

Emphasis on safety in both college and NFL games is a rising concern but it isn't new. In fact, the game was almost abolished in 1905 when 18 undergraduate players died from injuries. Harvard President Charles W. Eliot led a move to abolish the sport. The *New York Times* editorialized against "Two Curable Evils," lynching and football. Eliot might have succeeded but for the fact that Teddy Roosevelt was in the White House. The "first fan," our most muscular president, proclaimed the game "Bully!"

Roosevelt convened a 1906 White House meeting with the presidents of the three big Ivy League universities—Harvard, Princeton and Yale—and Walter Camp, the leading figure in the game's formative years.

Camp was a formidable personage, a peer to the others in that White House meeting. He had done more than refine the grunts of rugby into a more elegant but still bone-breaking sport. His basic rules distinguishing football from rugby created a more fluid game of 11-member squads, seven linemen and four backs, on a lined field, with four tries to go ten yards or surrender the ball. Camp had played for Yale and was inducted into Skull and Bones, the secret network of elites. He became chairman of a watch manufacturing company, wrote hundreds of articles for national publications such as *Harpers Weekly* and *Collier's*, advised the armed forces on physical fitness, and coached at Yale and later at Stanford.

According to John J. Miller, author of the definitive *The Great Scrum: How Teddy Roosevelt Saved Football*,

Roosevelt told the conferees: "Football is on trial. Because I believe in the game, I want to do all I can to save it." He acknowledged that real and permanent changes had to be made. One resultant change outlawed the flying wedge, whose human leading spear point, when it collided with the receiving team, was literally bone-crushing—and harkened back to the disciplined charge of Roman legions.

Another rules change was legalizing the forward pass. That change spread out the field and also lessened the number of violent crashes between young men in leather caps, contests whose absence of rules rivaled WWE SmackDowns. Out of TR's meeting grew the all-powerful, unsparing, unsmiling NCAA.

A cacophony of historians now claims to know who threw the first "illegal" forward pass, but my favorite candidate references man's most basic instinct. In a scoreless game between North Carolina and Georgia, the UNC punter caught the snap just as Georgia rushers broke through with unpleasant intentions. The panicked punter scurried to his right and threw the ball to the first teammate he saw, who sprinted 70 yards for a touchdown. Carolina won 6-0.

The Rise of Notre Dame

The perfection and popularity of the forward pass—and the rise of Notre Dame as a football power—can be traced to a summer on an Ohio beach. There, a Norwegian immigrant and Notre Dame left end named Knute Rockne was lifeguard. He and his roommate, All-American quarterback Gus Dorais, spent the summer creating a forward pass tandem. Rockne's path to fame was no series of summers on the beach. His father, a small-town Norwegian wagonmaker, immigrated to Chicago when Knute was five. To earn enough money to enroll at Notre Dame, Knute worked as a dispatcher for the post office until he was 22.

That summer's games of pass and catch between roommates was put to effective use in the fall. On Nov. 1, 1913, Coach Jesse Harper used the newly minted tandem against heavily favored Army. The threat of Dorais-to-Rockne deep passes kept Army from crowding the line of scrimmage. Dorais was 12 of 14 for 243 yards as a confused Army team went down 35-14.

After Rockne abandoned a career in chemistry to coach the Irish, yet another Army game was transfigured into the hall of legends. The team had fallen behind Army 6-0. At halftime Rockne reminded the team of the fabled George Gipp, who died of strep throat in 1920, two weeks after being named Notre Dame's second consensus All-American. Coach Rockne told his team what the Gipp had said on his deathbed: "I've got to go, Rock. It's all right. I'm not afraid. Some time, Rock, when the team is up against it, when things are going wrong and the breaks are beating the boys, tell them to go in there with all they've got and win just one for the Gipper. I don't know where I'll be then, Rock. But I'll know about it, and I'll be happy." An inspired team outscored Army in the second half and won 12-6.

In Rockne's 13 years coaching the Irish his record was 105 to 12, with 5 ties and three national championships. He was a national figure who, when he died in a plane crash at 43, was mourned by President Hoover and whose funeral was attended by a personal representative of Norway's King Haakon VII. Yet, through some strange spiritual transference, his story is associated more today with actor-cum-President Ronald Reagan who played the lead in the 1940 film *Knute Rockne, All American*. Reagan took possession of "The Gipper" nickname because of his emotional rendering of Rockne's locker room speech in the film.

Also now forgotten are the Notre Dame teams of Frank Leahy, 1941-53 with a won-loss percentage of .864, and Ara Parseghian, 1964-74 whose winning percentage of .836 had not been matched until now. A pall of mediocrity for two decades obscured Rockne's successor teams. Notre Dame had not won a title in 20 years or ranked in the top 10 until the 2012 season. This year it joined the ACC, a conference noted more for its basketball teams, but maintained partial independence in football so it could still line up against such regional powerhouses as the Purdue Boilermakers.

Notre Dame's glory in the early decades of collegiate football has been rekindled by a new, winning coach hired in December 2011. The 47-year-old Brian Kelly was 34-6 in three seasons at Cincinnati, leading the Bearcats to back-to-back Big East titles and two straight Bowl Championship Series berths. Before Kelly arrived to boost Notre Dame to its No. 1 AP ranking, the flickering memory of the Irish of yore was kept alive mainly by a continuing NBC contract to televise its home games.

STARS FELL ON ALABAMA

Since Nick Saban has taken up the mantle left by the secular saint Paul "Bear" Bryant, a strong argument can be made that Alabama has replaced the Irish as the national brand name. As fate would have it, Doug Walker, the assistant athletic director at Alabama, came to his position from Notre Dame. He says Alabama doesn't do anything special to promote itself: "Winning takes care of (projecting) the national brand" that "is built from decades of success." The SEC's contracts with CBS and ESPN also mean that several times a year Alabama blankets the nation—and beyond. Ken Gaddy, director of the Bryant Museum on the Alabama campus, likes to tell the story of an Argentinian who picked up the team on television and became such a fan that he named his restaurant "Alabama Café." Another indicator of the team's national fan base is the Collegiate Licensing Company, which ranks Alabama second only to Texas in recent royalties from merchandise sold.

Notre Dame's 2012 revival stirs anxieties for Bama fans, who are 1-5 against the Irish. Particularly bitter was the 1973 Sugar Bowl when an undefeated Tide was stalled by Coach Ara Parseghian's "mirror" defense; every option of the Alabama's vaunted wishbone offense was duplicated by the Notre Dame defense. A missed field goal by Alabama meant a 23-24 loss and only a share of the national title. Next year a replay with the Irish in the Orange Bowl produced a 13-11 victory for the Indiana team.

Coach Kelly's success promises to renew the rivalry as Notre Dame competes for its ninth national title. The

Tide, of course, can nonchalantly answer over its shoulder, "We're going for number 15; catch us if you can." And so it goes in the worshipful realm of the gridiron's civil religion.

Despite the locked-on loyalty of committed fans—I admit to being one—there are times when life intercedes to at least delay the feelings that precede the consummate moment, the kickoff for an important game. Late in the afternoon of the 2012 BCS Championship, I felt an unusual detachment, an almost agnostic attitude toward the contest of giants that would turn New Orleans's Superdome into a vast asylum for madmen, madwomen and even mad-children. I had spent the afternoon in concentrated study and editing which had left my brain on "empty," devoid of the usual sensations of anxiety or anticipation. When I finished my work and thoughts turned toward THE Game, fatalistic thoughts crawled through my conscious-ness, "What if LSU wins? I keep hearing on TV they're the better team and they probably will win. So what? It's only a game."

It was Red Bull time. My brain was too tired to resist heretical thoughts; something had to be done. But instead of cracking a can of the fizzy stimulant, I took a shower, put on my Bama shirt, and went downstairs to watch the hype. I felt so much better that it was even a pleasure to see the then-Auburn coach, Gene Chizik, as an analyst. He looked great in a gray striped suit, striped shirt with a white collar, and blazing yellow tie; he could have passed for a successful graduate of Alabama's law school.

The old feelings of anticipation mingled with anxiety

returned when the team ran onto the field—a crimson river flowing between the ranks of our fabled "Million Dollar Band." In my mind's eye I could see what a Birmingham sportswriter saw 100 years ago when the team played on a field of liquid mud and the reporter wrote they surged like a crimson tide. Except that this year the field where the band stood was as clean and green as a golf course.

Among the stories about the source of the band's name, the one I prefer is a remark attributed to World War I Commanding General John J. Pershing, who said army bands were worth "a million dollars" to troop morale. Of course, fans of other teams might prefer the story in Winston Groom's history of the team: an Atlanta sportswriter wrote that the team was lousy but the school had "a million dollar band."

Winning the halftime is good (and winning the postgame party even better) but the cosmic question was still who would win the national championship. Just before kickoff I was surprised to hear that overnight the Las Vegas odds had switched to favoring Alabama.   Could the gambling empire's agents have broken the Nick Saban code and uncovered the game plan? Did they know in advance that AJ McCarron would confound even the feared Honey Badger by throwing to the tight ends? Who could have guessed that Saban and Defensive Coordinator Kirby Smart could have crafted a defense that was a mirror image of everything LSU attempted, with even the scary option being devoured by a swarm of crimson amoebae.

In the end, LSU—the nation's yearlong unbeatable

No. 1 team—gained a total of 92 yards.

Alabama's execution was near-perfect excepting one out of six field goals and one extra point were missed. As the Tide's dominion over LSU worked its way to a 21-0 shutout and a 14th national championship, my earlier mental fatigue and spiking anxiety settled into a mood of calm contentment interrupted only by frequent fist-pumps and cheers.

The uncharitable might have defined Alabama fans' sense of wellbeing accompanying the victory as detestably smug. So be it; my conscience is clear. First, any endeavor that is crowned with being the very best in the nation is worthy of quiet admiration. Such a distinction is not achieved without hard work, planning and concentration. Though Nick Saban has proven to be one of the most gifted college coaches of all time, this team's story is not one of riches begetting riches; it is one of being scorned and with great effort rising to legendary status.

The nation's sportswriters had never heard of Alabama until President Mike Denny arranged to play the University of Pennsylvania in Philadelphia in 1922. It was then as un-expected for the presumed-shoeless Alabamians to compete on the national stage as it would be today for, say, Yale to defeat the Tide in Bryant-Denny stadium. Thus the sports world was shocked when Alabama beat Penn 9 to 7. Three years later the Rose Bowl Committee was so reluctant to invite the undefeated Tide that it asked three Ivy League teams before settling for Alabama against Washington. Not given a chance by West Coast newspapers, the Tide beat the Huskies 20-19 and won the national title. The next year the team tied Stanford 7-7 in the Rose Bowl and won the national title again.

The Tide won a third national title in 1930; white Protestants were rising to challenge the home team of every Catholic, Notre Dame, then a decade ahead in national prominence. The Tide's irritatingly regular triumphs in Pasadena, the last a 34-14 drubbing of Southern Cal in 1945, evidently convinced the Rose Bowl Committee to in effect ban the Tide by making the contest between the Pac 10 and Big 10.

Football Mutes Regional Insecurities

So, in the warm glow of another victory for a team that has striven and achieved, I was utterly without shame in January 2012 in uttering those immortal words: Roll Tide! They took the sting out of the result of the first "Game of the Century," when during the 2011 regular season No. 1 LSU met No. 2 Alabama—sunshine yellow and crimson flame on a green carpet, with pageantry to rival a Roman Festival. Such a feast of color, such a tournament of arms momentarily washes away cultural insecurities. Too, the magnificence of the sport itself, multi-splendored football, momentarily blots out any sense of inferiority, knowing we play the game better than high-church liberals of the Ivy League.

But the old ache was there. There is a nagging pain in the psychological center of Southern culture; an insecurity borne of damaged self-respect that is marbled through the emotion filling SEC stadiums on any Saturday night. You have to be born Southern, inheriting the region's Manichaean history of unrepentant sins and unacknowledged defeats, to recognize the feeling—melancholy cellos ominously humming deep beneath the triumphant brass of the bands, the color and the cheers.

It was there hidden in the elation of LSU fans on their regular-season 9-6 victory and in the heaviness of loss felt by depressed Tide partisans who believed, as I did, that the better team was done in by its own mistakes. But an LSU fan, in almost the same words an Alabamian would use, expressed the weeping wound in the South's psyche— "When we're No. 1, it's usually for something bad."

But put that aside; it is insignificant compared with the glories of football: merging the elegant artistry of ballet with the intelligence of chess; matching the grandeur of classic military campaigns with Shakespeare's tragedies; providing locker room speeches of timeless inspiration; occupying a high moral plane where rules and summary judgments are accepted without appeal. Further, college football is one of the region's great civil religions and among its most democratic activities, played and watched equally by blacks and whites, bankers and beauticians. It is the stage for magnificent pageantry of battalion-sized bands in colorful uniforms playing upbeat marches and of shapely cheerleaders, with perpetually beckoning smiles, who strike desire in the loins of undergraduate boys and the memories of older men.

Race relations bear special mention. So commonplace

is the mingling of the races among players and fans now that it is forgotten that football in the 1970s South was a fulcrum of social change and a display window to show how successful integration can be. The integration of the Crimson Tide is an example. The University itself had been desegregated since 1963 following Governor George C. Wallace's theatrical and futile attempt to block admission of two black students, Vivian Malone and James Hood. But though Bear Bryant favored integration, he was reluctant to tangle with Wallace and with troglodyte alumni. Perhaps he was also waiting for a deus ex machina at Legion Field to demonstrate the value of an integrated Tide.

He got not one but two gods to reveal the advantage of black players—University of Southern California running backs Sam "Bam" Cunningham and Clarence Davis who, between them, scored five touchdowns in USC's 42-21 demolition of the Tide in Birmingham in 1970. To punctuate the point, it was noted that Davis was a Birmingham native, having grown up within walking distance of Legion Field.

USC Coach John McKay did the Bear another favor with a tip about another black Alabamian, a terrific back named John Mitchell who was then playing junior college football in Arizona. Bryant recruited Mitchell to become the first African American to play football for the Tide. The next year, Mitchell became the team's first black co-captain, and the year after that, its first black assistant coach and also its youngest coach ever.

In recent years, it has not been unusual for Alabama—

or some other historically white SEC teams—to have 11 black players on the field at the same time, especially on defense. Bryant himself said that in his early career he liked to recruit tough, gangly impoverished white kids off the farms, because they were hungry. In his post-desegregation career, Bryant was fond of recruiting tough, gangly impoverished black kids from the inner cities, because, he said, they were hungry.

And it was not just at the college level that football in the early days of integration proved a fulcrum to help displace an ancient civilization. At previously white Notasulga High School in east Alabama, for example, black strangers were at first resented. But then the flagging fortunes of its football team reversed with new talent and the team—and town—began winning again. Victory can displace the most hardened prejudices.

It wasn't just the winning that made integration so swiftly accepted. It was also the bonding, on-the-field comrades looking out for one another...like soldiers. In sports, in the military, and in church, wherever people are bound together by a common goal or shared reverence, distinctions of race or station diminish. Football's significance as a civil religion is made manifest by its cathedrals of contest, which are set aside exclusively for that purpose, and its spiritual leaders, the coaches, are more revered and honored than mere bishops.

A Moral Equivalent

In football as in war—as in life—there is no place

for the timid and weak. We may pity the vulnerable who are broken by life, but we do not admire or follow them. Strong, hardy people who obey firm rules of conduct govern football, war, and life itself. The primary color of war and football is red—the color of intense emotion. John Keegan, the British military historian, came close to defining the spiritual force that moves men in sport as in war in this eloquent passage: "Warfare…reaches into the most secret places of the human heart, places where self dissolves rational purpose, where pride reigns, where emotion is paramount, where instinct is king."

Comparisons with actual combat ring so true. Students of military history know that the great Carthaginian general, Hannibal, invented plays such as the "draw" or "trap." It was at the town of Cannae, 216 BC, that the classic football sucker-play was invented.

Sixteen Roman legions attacked the Carthaginian. Hannibal stood with his men in the weak center and held them to a controlled retreat. Knowing the superiority of the Roman infantry, Hannibal had instructed his own infantry to withdraw. The Roman infantry drove deeper and deeper into the Carthaginian semicircle, forcing itself into an alley. At this decisive point, Hannibal ordered his African infantry waiting on the wings to turn inwards and advance against the Roman flanks, encircling the Roman infantry. The superior Roman force was slaughtered.

Defensive football tackles rushing through gaps in the offensive line and being blindsided by an offensive fullback know in a less deadly way how the Romans felt.

Such historic contests as the battles of Hastings in 1066 and Agincourt in 1415 foreshadowed then-Florida Coach Steve Spurrier's brilliant passing attack that used to win SEC championships. At Hastings, the invading Norman cavalry had outmaneuvered the Gene Stallings-like, stick-in-the-mud Anglo-Saxon ground troops. But cavalry met its match at Agincourt. Mysterious forces of will ignited by an unusually inspired leader affected that victory. One of the greatest locker room speeches of all time was that of Henry V's address to his men before Agincourt: "We few, we happy few / We band of brothers / For he to-day that sheds his blood with me / Shall be my brother / And gentlemen in England, now a-bed / Shall think themselves accursed they were not here / And hold their manhoods cheap whilst any speaks / That fought with us." Prince Hal's address to his troops ranks right up there with Knute Rockne's halftime "Gipper" speech at Notre Dame. Great warriors make great coaches.

There was nothing mysterious about English longbows whose practical effect was to decimate the French cavalry, firing long with pinpoint accuracy like a gifted quarterback throwing to designated spots on the field. In your mind's eye, follow the flight of a battalion of arrows arcing like distant birds until they fell, deadly points piercing man and horse. The French cavalry was destroyed.

Or…imagine the air war of Agincourt as it was translated at the University of Tennessee where Peyton Manning released the ball; it flies 10, 20, 30 yards, a beautiful spinning vessel, sun reflecting from its shiny leather, 90,000 fans holding their breath as it spirals down, 40 yards, 50 yards, and Peerless Price runs underneath for the catch. Touchdown!

If Hastings were a metaphor for a winning attack from the air, planned by a superior field general, then the Battle of Balaclava in 1854 during the Crimean War—popularly known as "the Charge of the Light Brigade"—is an example of tragically stupid coaching. Lord Ragland, overall commander of English forces, ordered a cavalry charge against what he thought were retreating Russian artillery. But since the obtuse general could not see the battlefield, the Light Brigade was sent into a valley whose hills on all sides were spiked with Russian cannon and riflemen. The senior cavalry commander, Lieutenant General the Earl of Lucan, who could see the battlefield clearly, gave the order to the commander of the Light Brigade, Major General the Earl of Cardigan, his brother-in-law who was bound to him in mutual hatred for decades. Despite his feelings for his brother-in-law, Cardigan obeyed, leading his lightly saber-armed cavalry directly into the Russian cannon—a charnal house of butchery. He then led the decimated few in retreat as the Russians continued to pour down shells. Having done all he could that day, with the nonchalance of a British gentleman going to his club, the general retired to his yacht for a champagne dinner.

Alfred, Lord Tennyson, then the poet laureate of the United Kingdom, dashed off what became an immortal poem after it was published in a popular newspaper. Among the most quoted lines are these:

'Forward, the Light Brigade!
Charge for the guns' he said:
Into the valley of Death
Rode the six hundred.
'Forward, the Light Brigade!'
Was there a man dismay'd?
Not tho' the soldiers knew
Some one had blunder'd:
Theirs not to make reply,
Theirs not to reason why,
Theirs but to do and die:
Into the valley of Death
Rode the six hundred.

A more contemporary example of bad generalship was Douglas MacArthur—a latter-day Lord Ragland—running the Korean War from Japan. One of the favored generals in Emperor MacArthur's court, Lieutenant General Ned Almond, like a coach who fails to study films of his opponents, did not appreciate the scale of the hordes of Chinese sweeping down from the north. He advised a Marine general under his command, "The enemy who is delaying you for the moment is nothing more than remnants of Chinese divisions fleeing north. We're still attacking and we're going all the way to the Yalu. Don't let a bunch of Chinese laundrymen stop you." The Marine general disobeyed and his division escaped. Almond's X Corps was defeated.

A coach who prepared his team to defend a passing

attack, ignoring a devastating ground game would find his equivalent in the personally impressive General Maxwell Taylor, who guided his forces in Vietnam against an invisible insurgency as if the Viet Cong were massed German divisions. More men and boys died than necessary because of the bad judgment of their leaders.

It seems somehow wrong to equate unimaginable, insane courage with sport. But it is possible to replicate the same mixture of obtuseness, stupidity, and reckless courage on the football field. If stupidity and spite that cost the lives of British and American soldiers is a source of Vesuvian anger, then the stupidity of coaches who crushed the hope and realistic expectations of teenagers and young men, leaving some injured, is just a matter of degree. It has happened, sparking angry disappointment—yet another source of the passion we invest in the sport.

What Hannibal did to the Roman infantry became the title of a popular film, *The Blind Side*, which I've seen three times, compelled by the plot's contradictions and surprises: the upper-income Memphis family who took in a homeless black teenager, made him part of the family, and inspired him to All-American and NFL football glory. Reviewers from other parts of the country, who lack the attic full of contradictory insights that a Southerner brings to the film, might be tempted to dismiss it as standard feel-good, pop psychology, but hardly believable. A wealthy, white, Republican family taking in a gigantic, ill-clothed, taciturn black child abandoned by a drug-addicted mother, sending him to a white Christian prep school, where he stars on the football team and goes on to be the All-American tackle Michael Oher for Ole Miss? Yeah, right.

That path leads inevitably to a sociological tangle of class and race, a thicket perfectly designed to obscure meaning. Southerners and anyone with an open mind would know what was going on and that it is more important than white or black, wealth or poverty.

The line that summarizes the movie's incongruous bond is, "Who would have guessed that we would have a black son before we met a Democrat?" Sandra Bullock takes over the movie, carving out a character who can purr or snap orders, who has veins of iron and generosity as wide as the Mississippi; she elevates "steel magnolia" to a new level of complexity. She is so sexy, so tough, so smart about simple human nature that she makes a better high school coach than the dimwit with the whistle. She is so good that she almost overwhelms major supporting actors, football, and Ole Miss.

ABIDING VALUES OF WAR

The fabled Ohio State coach Woody Hayes fed on a diet of military history and Shakespeare's tragedies. George Will once wrote that he could imagine Hayes in Columbus on a blustery fall day, roaming the sidelines in a Shakespearean rage, muttering, "Blow winds, and crack your cheeks!" The quote is from King Lear, when the old king is beset by storms, demons within stronger than the tempest outside. The stormy scene is right, but Will chose the wrong king. Lear was weak. He divided his kingdom among his children to gain their love, which caused civil war among the siblings.

It is unthinkable to imagine Hayes or Bear Bryant abandoning his authority to win the affection of assistant coaches, thus precipitating destructive rivalry among the staff. Woody Hayes was successful because he filled his mind with Shakespeare's insights into human character, and the great battles of history. He had seen combat himself in World War II, his last command a destroyer escort, and he knew that battle teaches the values of obedience, discipline, camaraderie, courage under fire, and the unpredictability of Fate.

Woody Hayes's approach to football was summed up by author and theologian Michael Novak who, with apologies to William James, put it this way: "If war is the teacher men have turned to in order to learn teamwork, discipline, coolness under fire, respect for contingency and fate, football is my moral equivalent of war."

In his essay, William James said that any moral equivalent to war, such as a term of military service for the young, should inculcate strong values: "Martial virtues must be the enduring cement; intrepidity, contempt of softness, surrender of private interest, obedience to command, must still remain the rock upon which states are built…"

The founder of NFL Films, Ed Sabol, was inspired to create films of martial majesty. Sabol was sitting on his helmet in a field outside Paris in 1944 when General George S. Patton spoke, motivating his troops for battle, erasing their memories of civil life, turning them into warriors.

"Courage is fear holding out a minute longer. No bastard ever won a war dying for his country. He won it by making the other poor dumb bastard die for his country." Patton's confidence and showmanship, the whip and antique pistols, impressed young Sabol. "…We were terrified, but he was magnificent, a real showman. He knew how important the theatrical things are at the brutal moments. As long as he was talking we weren't afraid."

Watching films produced by Sabol and his late son Steve, you can almost see Patton in the form of Vince Lombardi, "Winning isn't everything, it's the only thing." In one film a convoy of guards block for a Green Bay halfback's wondrous touchdown run, convoyed, too, by background symphonic music: Richard Wagner's magnificent swelling, whirring "Ride of the Valkyries." The writing, the editing and choice of music in NFL films lent a majesty to the game—football as high art.

Civil Religion, or the Real Thing

Football is, as noted above, a principle civil religion of this region. But there is so much more. Michael Novak could have been describing a quarterback and a team in a transcendent moment of perfection when he wrote in his *Joy of Sports* the following: "To keep cool, to handle hundreds of details and call exactly the plays that work, to fight one's way through opposition to do what one wills to do, against odds, against probabilities—these are to practice a very high art, to achieve a few moments of beauty…a form eternal in its beauty. It is as though muscle and nerves and spirit and comrades were working together as flawlessly as God once imagined human beings might."

When Michael was researching *Joy of Sports*, I invited him to an Alabama-Auburn game in the era when Legion Field was divided into two equal and equally hostile crowds facing each other across the field. Afterwards, he said that Big 10 games were like attending a Unitarian Church service but "this was evangelical."

It is alleged that some of the fervor exhibited by fans is fired by something stronger than communion wine. A story is told about one fan's behavior at the bizarre upset of Auburn over Alabama at the "Iron Bowl," as the inter-state rivalry is known, on Dec. 2, 1972. With less than ten minutes to go Alabama, undefeated and ranked No. 2 nationally, was in control of the game, 16 to 3. Auburn's defense forced the Tide to punt but the punt was blocked by Bill Newton and picked up by David Langner who ran it in for an Auburn touchdown. Minutes later – incredibly—Newton blocked another punt, which Langner again retrieved and scored. Auburn won the shocker, 17-16. After the final seconds ticked off, an unvanquished Bama fan in an aisle seat rose to give a lusty "Roll Tide," waving a bottle half filled with dark liquid. He stumbled and rolled several aisles, hugging the bottle as if it were a football, and rose uninjured to shout, "We lost the game but we're gonna win the party." I was there, unfortunately more sober than he.

It was an unforgettable contest, made so by Auburn fans taunting, for years after, "Punt Bama, Punt."

Which raises the question: Why do we care so intensely

about a game, hold our breath until a pass is caught or dropped, experience hours of tension so intense as to cause headaches? The fan is exhibiting a form of patriotism, which is no simple thing. For each fan the feeling is singular and original; the team, in its distinctive colors running onto the field, awakens a cluster of emotional memories. All packed together, it is family, home, grade-school classmates singing "God Bless America" joyously off key, the anxiety of the college freshman too soon becoming the nostalgia of an old grad. It is all of life's experiences that produce bursts of exultation and fits of despondency that define us—as football fans.

Irritating though the Auburn fans' yells of "Punt, Bama, Punt" may be, I prefer them to the smug superiority of those who disparage the game. There is about them the suspicion that life has coddled rather than tested them. Those who have not known disappointment or defeat, who haven't experienced frustration and the pain of good, hard, repeated smacks—they live on a plane above common humanity. I never met one I truly liked; they make me wonder what they know of life. What do they have to teach, what do they feel, what moves them?

Give me the raucous fan who bleeds Alabama crimson or Auburn orange and blue or Notre Dame gold and blue; they are real. You know where they come from and the church where they worship. The congregants are bound to one another through faith in a presence larger than self, which for the truly devout allows them to believe they are blessed, enlarged by their faith. It is not an ecumenical religion. The liturgy is sect-specific and exclusive: Those who worship at the shrine of Saint Bear never utter the prayer, "War Eagle!" Neither do those martyred in service to the Apostles of the Plains allow a "Roll Tide" to pass their lips.

Faithful loyalty to the team has been raised to an evangelical, proselyting mission. In the Virginia foothills faith-based, burgeoning Liberty University's ambition is to bring the world to Christ — through football.

Evangelism, however, can't reach potential converts in sufficient numbers unless the pulpit sits on a national stage. That high pulpit was the vision of Liberty's founder, the late Jerry Falwell of Moral Majority fame, which is being carried on by his son, Jerry Jr., the school's chancellor. "Football's role in making Liberty a national institution was my father's vision from the very beginning," he told Bill Pennington of The New York Times.

The elder Falwell imagined Liberty vs. Notre Dame, a rivalry of Catholics against Protestants, those echoes again of the Reformation and Thirty Years War. Turner Gill, a former Nebraska All-American and Kansas University coach hired last year to build up the Liberty program, saw dual potential to attaining major power status: one, making the 82,000 online students feel part of the institution through televised games, and the primary goal, "God has called us to be examples and to change the world," he said. "We can touch millions."

Is Falwell Senior's dream totally outlandish: a former Bible college winning games and winning souls to Christ in great cathedrals filled with tens of thousands, voices uplifted, "Onward Christian Soldiers…"

Not really. For one thing, Liberty is prosperous; its online university has mushroomed its assets by $900 million over the past five years.

Carr Sports Consulting of Gainesville, Florida, hired to direct the build-up, believes it can succeed. "They are a quantum leap ahead of any school we've worked with," said Bill Carr. "Liberty is the best-prepared and has, by far, the most resources. It's simply a matter of time before they get there."

It is not out of the question that, with enough money and determination, Liberty can recruit squads of Tebows and have a nationally competitive football team. But it is its self-defined role as savior of the world's soul that is grandiosely inflated.

Liberty is not The Church of football; it is a denomination. Falwell's fundamental error is regarding football as a mere vehicle. It is not; it is greater than Liberty. Football IS the religion itself, which all other denominations worship on Saturday.

Faith for some persuades them that their papal leader can perform miracles. It was claimed that during his 25 years and six national championships that Paul W. "Bear" Bryant coached at Alabama that he could walk on water. The Bear had heard and no doubt enjoyed the supernatural compliment. At the conclusion of a pilgrimage to his birthplace in Morro Bottom, near Fordyce, Arkansas, an occasion which had been cooked up by sportswriters, broadcasters, and some former players, when the "pilgrims" formed a semicircle around the decaying, derelict house, they fell into an embarrassed silence. Then one broke the mood, joking, "Bear, I thought you were born in a log cabin." The Bear growled, "Naw, that was Lincoln. I was born in…a manger."

Other faiths have their own myths, mysteries and miracles, but they all have their sacred music. Just as the lively Baptist hymns differ from those in the Episcopal hymnal, the fight songs of rival universities differ in originality, tempo, and meaning. Contrast the hymns of traditional rivals Alabama and Tennessee.

As maddening as it may be to hear the anthem of a different faith played incessantly during the service at such temples as Neyland Stadium, "Rocky Top" is not only a catchy tune but is rich in the cultural traditions of the Appalachian South. It is a lament for the loss of a simpler way of life and a hymn to the folkways of the hill South. It speaks of clean air free of smoky smog and telephone bills, dreams of a mountain woman half bear and half cat, wild as a mink but sweet as a soda pop, and notes that corn doesn't grow in rocky soil and that's why "they get their likker in a jar." The song was played on its 40th anniversary on the third Saturday in October 2012, the traditional date of the Alabama-Tennessee game. The end of its plaintive hankering for home and an uncomplicated life goes:

> I've had years of cramped-up city life
> Trapped like a duck in a pen
> All I know is it's a pity life

Can't be simple again
Rocky Top, you'll always be
Home sweet home to me
Good ol' Rocky Top
Rocky Top Tennessee,
Rocky Top Tennessee

Alabama's favorite, "Yea Alabama," is more straightforward, no fooling around with former girl friends or nostalgia for lost innocence. It is a no-nonsense statement of the values of football now—winning—and a projection into the future. The song was written in 1926 by Lundy Sykes, then editor of the campus newspaper. Sykes composed the song in response to a contest to create a fight song following Alabama's first Rose Bowl victory. It goes:

Yea, Alabama! Drown 'em Tide!
Every Bama Man's behind you, hit your stride!
Go teach the Bulldogs to behave!
Send the Yellow Jackets to a Watery Grave!
And if a man starts to weaken, that's his shame:
For Bama's pluck and grit
Have writ her name in Crimson Flame.
Fight on! Fight on! Fight on, men!
Remember the Rose Bowl, we'll win then.
Go, roll to vict'ry! Hit your stride!
You're Dixie's football pride, Crimson Tide!

Just as men have forever marched off to war with bands

playing, so have soldiers of the gridiron pouring onto the field been greeted with sprightly renditions of the school's songs. If Clausewitz is correct in his theory that war is a continuation of politics by different means, man continually has war on his mind. The early 19th-century Prussian general had a practical sense of how chance and misjudgements, for instance, might affect the conduct of "politics."

The U.S. has been at war four times in my lifetime, justly and nobly only once, in World War II. There are no bands playing and flags waving in the freezing, frightened, muddy, insect-bitten bowels of combat; similarly the school fight song sounds tinny in a rain-soaked, losing match against a superior team.

But man forever craves the matching of muscle and will. War like football is a joyous thing at the start. And winning, what glory there is in winning.

♣

FROM THE SAME AUTHOR —

The journey of writer and publisher H. Brandt Ayers took him from the segregated Old South to a newly minted civilization, the New South, in which he had a leadership role. As a young reporter and editor, he covered the crucible of the civil rights struggle in Raleigh, Washington, and—as editor of his family's newspaper, the ANNISTON STAR—in his own hometown.

"Brandt Ayers has come as close as anybody ever has to explaining who we Southerners are and why we act as we do." —Governor William Winter

IN LOVE WITH DEFEAT

The Making of a Southern Liberal

H. BRANDT AYERS

Ayers's journey was one of controversy and danger, including coverage of a racist nightrider murder and taut moments when the community teetered on the edge of mob violence. His narrative has outsized figures from U.S. Attorney General Robert Kennedy to George Wallace, including probing insights into the Alabama governor as he evolved over time.

Ayers sees the birth of a New South movement, the election of a Southern president, and the strange undoing of that presidency. The South is also mirrored in diplomatic and journalistic ventures into other nations with histories as hard or harder than that of the South: Russia, China, and South Africa.

An afterword, made imperative by the cultural and political exclamation point of a black president, bridges the years from the disappearance of the New South in the 1980s to Barack Obama's first term.

Order online at www.newsouthbooks.com/ayers
ISBN 978-1-58838-277-1, hardcover, $29.95
ISBN 978-1-60306-107-0, ebook, $9.99